February/Febrero

By/Por Robyn Brode

Reading Consultant/Consultora de lectura: Linda Cornwell,
Literacy Connections Consulting/consultora de lectoescritura

WEEKLY READER®
PUBLISHING

Please visit our web site at **www.garethstevens.com**.
For a free catalog describing our list of high-quality books, call 1-800-542-2595 (USA) or 1-800-387-3178 (Canada). Our fax: 1-877-542-2596

Library of Congress Cataloging-in-Publication Data
Brode, Robyn.
    [February. Spanish & English]
    February / by Robyn Brode ; reading consultant, Linda Cornwell — Febrero / por Robyn Brode ; consultora de lectura, Linda Cornwell.
       p. cm. — (Months of the year — Meses del año)
    English and Spanish in parallel text.
    Includes bibliographical references and index.
    ISBN-10: 1-4339-1930-3   ISBN-13: 978-1-4339-1930-5 (lib. bdg.)
    ISBN-10: 1-4339-2107-3   ISBN-13: 978-1-4339-2107-0 (softcover)
    1. February—Juvenile literature.   2. Holidays—United States—Juvenile literature.
    3. Winter—United States—Juvenile literature.   I. Cornwell, Linda. II. Title. III. Title: Febrero.
    GT4803.B765   2010b
    394.261—dc22   2009013359

This edition first published in 2010 by
Weekly Reader® Books
An Imprint of Gareth Stevens Publishing
1 Reader's Digest Road
Pleasantville, NY 10570-7000 USA

Copyright © 2010 by Gareth Stevens, Inc.

Executive Managing Editor: Lisa M. Herrington
Senior Editors: Barbara Bakowski, Jennifer Magid-Schiller
Designer: Jennifer Ryder-Talbot
Translators: Tatiana Acosta and Guillermo Gutiérrez

Photo Credits: Cover, back cover, title © Ariel Skelley/Weekly Reader; p. 7 © SW Productions/Weekly Reader; p. 9 © Image Source/SuperStock; p. 11 © blue jean images/Getty Images; p. 13 (top left) © Courtesy of Barack Obama's Senate office; p. 13 (top right) © Don Cravens/Time & Life Pictures/Getty Images; p. 13 (bottom left) © J. R. Eyerman/Time & Life Pictures/Getty Images; p. 13 (bottom right) © Astrid Stawiarz/Getty Images; p. 15 © Jupiter Images; p. 17 © Terrie L. Zeller/Shutterstock; p. 19 (left & right) © AP Images; p. 21 © Fotoret/Shutterstock

Printed in the United States of America

1 2 3 4 5 6 7 8 9 10 11 10 09

Table of Contents/Contenido

Boldface words appear in the glossary.

Las palabras en **negrita** aparecen en el glosario.

Welcome to February!

February is the second month of the year. It is the shortest month. February usually has 28 days.

-- -- -- -- -- -- -- --

¡Bienvenidos a febrero!

Febrero es el segundo mes del año. Es el mes más corto. Febrero suele tener 28 días.

Months of the Year/Meses del año

Month/Mes	Number of Days/ Días en el mes
1 January/Enero	31
2 February/Febrero	**28 or 29*/28 ó 29***
3 March/Marzo	31
4 April/Abril	30
5 May/Mayo	31
6 June/Junio	30
7 July/Julio	31
8 August/Agosto	31
9 September/Septiembre	30
10 October/Octubre	31
11 November/Noviembre	30
12 December/Diciembre	31

*February has an extra day every fourth year./Febrero tiene un día extra cada cuatro años. **5**

Every four years, February has an extra day. The fourth year is called a **leap year**.

– – – – – – – – – –

Cada cuatro años, febrero tiene un día extra. A ese cuarto año lo llamamos **año bisiesto**.

February/Febrero

				1	2	3
4	5	6	7	8	9	10
11	12	13	14	15	16	17
18	19	20	21	22	23	24
25	26	27	28	(29)		

Winter Weather

February is a **winter** month. It might be cold or warm where you live.

- - - - - - - - - -

Tiempo de invierno

Febrero es uno de los meses de **invierno**. Según el lugar donde vivas, puede hacer frío o hacer buen tiempo.

What do you like to do outside in February?

- - - - - - - -

¿Qué te gusta hacer al aire libre en febrero?

8

Special Celebrations

In some years, Chinese New Year begins in February. Red **envelopes** are given as gifts. The envelopes have "lucky money" inside.

– – – – – – – – – –

Celebraciones especiales

Algunos años, el Año Nuevo Chino empieza en febrero. Como regalo, se entregan unos **sobres** rojos. En los sobres hay "dinero de la suerte".

envelope/sobre

11

February is Black History Month. It is time to learn about famous African Americans.

— — — — — — — — —

Febrero es el Mes de la Historia Afroamericana. Es un buen momento para conocer mejor a algunos afroamericanos famosos.

 Which other famous African Americans will you honor this month?

— — — — — — —

¿A qué otros afroamericanos famosos recordamos este mes?

Barack Obama
U.S. president/presidente
de Estados Unidos

Rosa Parks
civil rights leader/líder
de los derechos civiles

Jackie Robinson
baseball player/jugador
de béisbol

Oprah Winfrey
talk show host/presentadora
de televisión

13

February 2 is Groundhog Day. People say that if a **groundhog** sees its shadow on this day, winter will last six more weeks. If no shadow is seen, spring will be early.

- - - - - - - - - -

El 2 de febrero es el Día de la Marmota. La gente cree que si una **marmota** ve su sombra ese día, el invierno durará seis semanas más. Si no ve su sombra, la primavera llegará antes.

groundhog/
marmota

February Holidays

February 14 is called **Valentine's Day**. Friends, family, and classmates give each other cards and gifts.

– – – – – – – – – –

Fiestas de febrero

El 14 de febrero es el **Día de San Valentín**. Amigos, familiares y compañeros de clase se intercambian tarjetas y regalos.

Presidents' Day is a holiday that honors two famous presidents. Both George Washington and Abraham Lincoln were born in February.

– – – – – – – – – –

El Día de los Presidentes es una fiesta en honor de dos famosos presidentes. George Washington y Abraham Lincoln nacieron en febrero.

George Washington,
1st U.S. president/
primer presidente de
Estados Unidos

Abraham Lincoln,
16th U.S. president/
presidente número 16 de
Estados Unidos

When February ends, March begins. Soon it will be spring.

— — — — — — — — —

Cuando febrero termina, empieza marzo. Pronto llegará la primavera.

Glossary/Glosario

envelopes: flat containers for letters

groundhog: a small, furry animal that sleeps through the winter

leap year: a year that has 366 days. Every fourth year, February has an extra day.

Valentine's Day: February 14, a day to send cards and gifts to special people

winter: the season between fall and spring. It is usually the coldest time of the year.

▬ ▬ ▬ ▬ ▬ ▬ ▬ ▬ ▬ ▬

año bisiesto: año que tiene 366 días. Cada cuatro años, febrero tiene un día extra.

Día de San Valentín: el 14 de febrero, un día en que la gente envía tarjetas y regalos a sus seres queridos

invierno: la estación del año entre el otoño y la primavera. Suele ser la época más fría del año.

marmota: animal pequeño y peludo que duerme durante el invierno

sobres: cubiertas para enviar cartas

For More Information/Más información

Books/Libros

Presidents' Day/Día de los presidentes. Our Country's Holidays/ Las fiestas de nuestra nación (series). Sheri Dean (Gareth Stevens Publishing, 2006)

Winter/Invierno. Seasons of the Year/Las estaciones del año (series). JoAnn Early Macken (Gareth Stevens Publishing, 2006)

Web Sites/Páginas web

African American Biographies/Biografías de afroamericanos
www.factmonster.com/spot/afroambios.html
Read about famous African Americans in history./Conozcan a famosos personajes históricos afroamericanos.

White House 101/La Casa Blanca 101
www.whitehouse.gov/kids/presidentsday
Learn about the presidents of the United States./Encuentren información sobre los presidentes de Estados Unidos.

Index/Índice

About the Author

Robyn Brode has been a teacher, a writer, and an editor in the book publishing field for many years. She earned a bachelor's degree in English literature from the University of California, Berkeley.

Información sobre la autora

Robyn Brode ha sido maestra, escritora y editora de libros durante muchos años. Obtuvo su licenciatura en literatura inglesa en la Universidad de California, Berkeley.